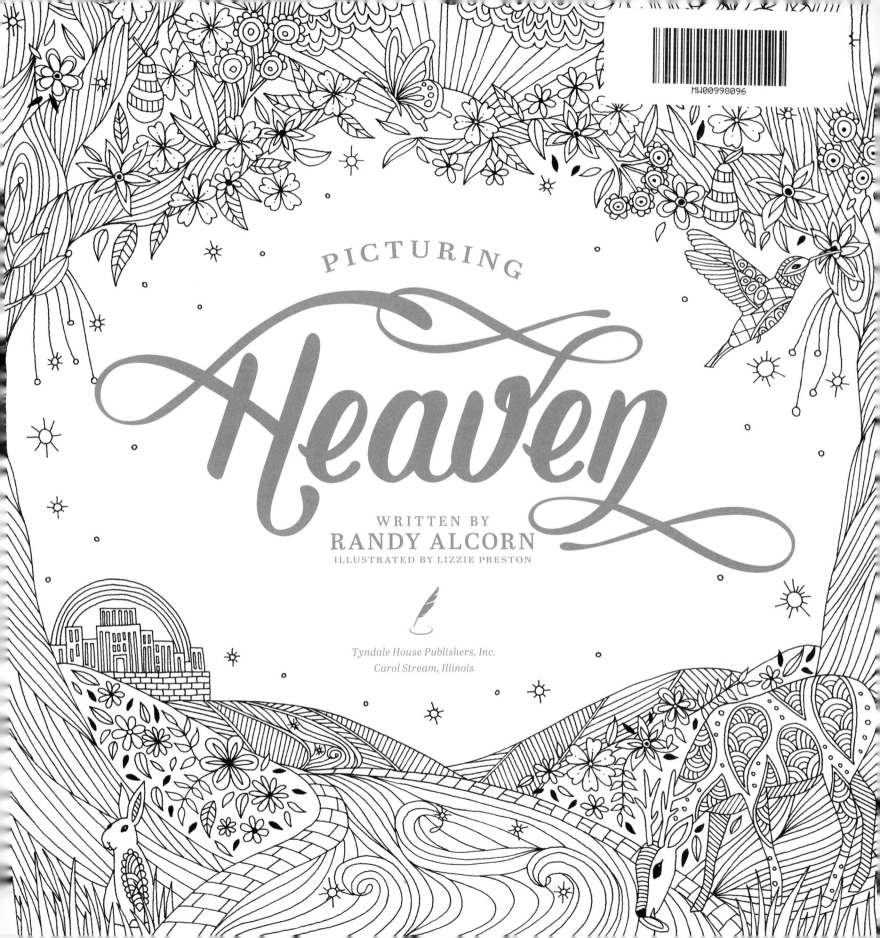

PICTURING

Heaven

WRITTEN BY
RANDY ALCORN
ILLUSTRATED BY LIZZIE PRESTON

Tyndale House Publishers, Inc.
Carol Stream, Illinois

Living Expressions invites you to explore God's Word and express your creativity in ways that are refreshing to the spirit and restorative to the soul.

LIVING
EXPRESSIONS™
COLLECTION

Visit Tyndale online at www.tyndale.com.

Visit the author's website at www.epm.org.

TYNDALE and Tyndale's quill logo are registered trademarks of Tyndale House Publishers, Inc. *Living Expressions* is a trademark of Tyndale House Publishers, Inc.

Picturing Heaven: 40 Hope-Filled Devotions with Coloring Pages

Devotions adapted from *Heaven*, copyright © 2004 by Eternal Perspective Ministries; *50 Days of Heaven*, copyright © 2006 by Eternal Perspective Ministries; and *We Shall See God*, copyright © 2011 by Eternal Perspective Ministries. New text copyright © 2017 by Eternal Perspective Ministries. All rights reserved.

Cover illustration by Lizzie Preston. Copyright © by Tyndale House Publishers, Inc. All rights reserved.

Interior illustrations by Lizzie Preston and Jennifer Tucker. Copyright © by Tyndale House Publishers, Inc. All rights reserved.

Designed by Jennifer Ghionzoli

Unless otherwise indicated, all Scripture quotations are taken from the *Holy Bible*, New Living Translation, copyright © 1996, 2004, 2015 by Tyndale House Foundation. Used by permission of Tyndale House Publishers, Inc., Carol Stream, Illinois 60188. All rights reserved.

Scripture quotations marked CEB are taken from the Common English Bible, copyright © 2011. All rights reserved.

Scripture quotations marked ESV are taken from *The Holy Bible*, English Standard Version® (ESV®), copyright © 2001 by Crossway, a publishing ministry of Good News Publishers. Used by permission. All rights reserved.

Scripture quotations marked GNT are taken from the Good News Translation in Today's English Version, Second Edition, copyright © 1992 by American Bible Society. Used by permission.

Scripture quotations marked NCV are taken from the New Century Version.® Copyright © 2005 by Thomas Nelson, Inc. Used by permission. All rights reserved.

Scripture quotations marked NIV are taken from the Holy Bible, *New International Version*,® NIV.® Copyright © 1973, 1978, 1984, 2011 by Biblica, Inc.® (Some quotations may be from the earlier NIV edition, copyright © 1984.) Used by permission. All rights reserved worldwide.

Scripture verses marked *Phillips* are taken from *The New Testament in Modern English* by J. B. Phillips, copyright © J. B. Phillips, 1958, 1959, 1960, 1972. All rights reserved.

For information about special discounts for bulk purchases, please contact Tyndale House Publishers at csresponse@tyndale.com, or call 1-800-323-9400.

ISBN 978-1-4964-2527-0

Printed in China

25 24 23 22 21 20 19
8   7   6   5   4   3

To
DOREEN BUTTON,
who played a vital role in helping put this book together,
and to Life Impact, the ministry she serves.

No eye has seen, no ear has heard,
and no mind has imagined what
God has prepared for those who love him.

— ❧ —

But it was to us that God revealed these things by his Spirit.

1 CORINTHIANS 2:9-10

CONTENTS

Introduction 9

1 From Better to Best—Our True Destination 10

2 Earth's End Will Lead to Earth's New Beginning 12

3 Earth Will Become the Paradise God Intended 14

4 Welcome Home to God's New Earth! 16

5 Heaven on Earth—God Will Make Our Home His 18

6 Resurrected People Living on a Resurrected Earth 20

7 Experiencing the Best of Eden 22

8 The New Jerusalem—A Reservoir of Wealth and Treasure 24

9 Eternal Freedom from Sorrow 26

10 Lasting Rest after Our Present Hardships 28

11 Remembering Christ's Sacrifice Will Forever Enhance Our Happiness 30

12 Everlasting Reasons to Celebrate 32

13 Seeking Heaven and Getting Earth Thrown In 34

14 Heaven's Gates Are Open Wide to All of God's People 36

15 A City with All of the Fun and None of the Sin 38

16 Earth's Present Beauty: Just a Hint of What's to Come 40

17 See the Sea in a Whole New Way 42

18 Weather on the New Earth? Why Not! 44

19 At Last, We'll Have Time for Everything 46

20 Spend Eternity Exploring Creation with Jesus 48

21 Get Ready to Join the Feast 50

22 Delighting in Redeemed Culture 52

23 Want to Share a Steaming Cup with Our Savior? 54

24 Lions and Lambs Will Be Our Gentle Companions 56

25 Will We Reunite with Our Beloved Pets? 58

26 Maybe We'll See Extinct Animals Come to Life 60

27 No Boredom in Heaven 62

28 Enjoy Activities You've Never Before Dared 64

29 Will We Travel to Galaxies Far, Far Away? 66

30 Our Greatest Joy Made Greater 68

31 God Takes Pleasure in Giving Us His Gifts 70

32 Service and Work as They Were Meant to Be 72

33 Universal Peace and Unity 74

34 Hospitality as We've Never Known It Before 76

35 Dance and Sing like Nobody's Watching 78

36 Leap for Joy and Laugh with Jesus 80

37 Humble Workers Will Gain Rich Rewards 82

38 Our Best Efforts May Find a Place in the New Creation 84

39 No More Pain, Tears, or Death 86

40 Anticipating Our Heavenly Rewards 88

Acknowledgments 91

About the Author 93

Sketches 94

Notes 95

THE SUBJECT OF HEAVEN gripped my interest when my mother was dying of cancer in 1981. As I've studied and spoken on this topic over the years, it's become clear that many in the church haven't yet fully grasped what Scripture teaches. Most Christians are familiar with the present Heaven, the place where we as believers in Jesus go to live when our physical bodies die.

Yet when the Bible promises Heaven, it also promises something bigger and everlasting, when God will resurrect our bodies *and* the earth. God Himself will come down to live with us forever—on the New Earth (Revelation 21:3). This is the ultimate Heaven that God's people eagerly anticipate: "We are looking forward to the new heavens and new earth he has promised, a world filled with God's righteousness" (2 Peter 3:13).

People can only look forward to what they can imagine, what they can picture in their mind's eye. Unfortunately, many have vague, dreary, and unbiblical notions that cause them to dread Heaven rather than long for it. The more tangible the New Earth becomes to us, the more we'll look forward to it.

That's perhaps the greatest value of this book: Coloring the imagery—trees, lakes, animals, and people enjoying a redeemed creation—will help you develop a vital view of the magnificent New Earth God is preparing for us! As you ponder these pictures and participate in the art, you'll more fully appreciate Christ's promise—not of a ghostly existence, but of resurrected bodies and minds in a fantastically beautiful, resurrected universe ruled by Jesus, the King of kings, our Savior and Lord.

My prayer is that *Picturing Heaven* will serve as both a creative expression and a spiritual inspiration. My desire is that the art, the Scripture, and my brief devotional thoughts will broaden your perspective, increase your hope, and nourish your faith. Perhaps one day when you're with Jesus, you'll look around and say, "This is what I imagined while coloring *Picturing Heaven*—and it's way better than I dreamed!"

Randy Alcorn

FROM BETTER TO BEST—OUR TRUE DESTINATION

I'm torn between two desires: I long to go and be with Christ, which would be far better for me. But for your sakes, it is better that I continue to live.

PHILIPPIANS 1:23-24

"As surely as my new heavens and earth will remain, so will you always be my people, with a name that will never disappear," says the Lord.

ISAIAH 66:22

THE PRESENT HEAVEN, where believers in Jesus go when their physical bodies die, is where we'll dwell prior to our bodily resurrection. Scripture says that to live there is "far better" than living here on Earth under the Curse, away from the direct presence of God. Still, the present Heaven is not our journey's end. Though it will be a wonderful place, it is not the place we are made for. There's another place God promises to refashion for us to live in forever. God's children are destined for life as resurrected beings on a resurrected Earth. We must not lose sight of our true destination!

EARTH'S END WILL LEAD TO EARTH'S NEW BEGINNING

The day of the Lord will come as unexpectedly as a thief.
Then the heavens will pass away with a terrible noise,
and the very elements themselves will disappear in fire,
and the earth and everything on it will be found to deserve judgment.

2 PETER 3:10

THIS VERSE about the earth's destruction can be misunderstood unless we catch what Peter says three verses later: "We are looking forward to the new heavens and new earth he has promised, a world filled with God's righteousness" (2 Peter 3:13). The same Earth destined for destruction is also destined for renewal. Many have grasped the first teaching but not the second. Therefore, they misinterpret phrases such as "pass away" or "disappear in fire" to mean final destruction rather than what Scripture actually teaches: a temporary destruction that will be reversed through resurrection. As great artists have restored ruined canvases, God will remake the charred Earth into something fresh and vibrant, greater than the original, just as a butterfly is greater than a caterpillar.

EARTH WILL BECOME THE PARADISE GOD INTENDED

God looked over all he had made, and he saw that it was very good!

GENESIS 1:31

RECONCILE. *Redeem. Restore. Recover. Return. Renew. Regenerate. Resurrect.* Each of these biblical words begins with the *re-* prefix, suggesting a return to an original condition that was ruined or lost. These words emphasize that God always sees us in light of the purpose He envisioned for us, and He always seeks to *restore us* to that design. Likewise, He sees Earth in terms of what He intended it to be, and He will restore it to its original design. Jesus called this the coming "renewal of all things" (Matthew 19:28, NIV).

WELCOME HOME TO GOD'S NEW EARTH!

My Father's house has many rooms . . .
I am going there to prepare a place for you.

JOHN 14:2, NIV

JESUS DELIBERATELY CHOSE common physical terms (*house, rooms, place*) to describe where He was going and what He was preparing. He wanted to give His disciples, and us, something tangible to look forward to—an actual place, a *home*, where we can go to be with Him. Not an ethereal realm of disembodied spirits, because such a place could never be home for us. Rather, this home will be a place that's both physical and spiritual, just as we are. A place that's a renewed version of the original one God made for us: Earth. Your new home, liberated from sin, curse, and suffering, is nearly ready for you. Moving day is coming.

- 5 -

I saw a throne in heaven and someone sitting on it.

The one sitting on the throne was as brilliant as gemstones—like jasper

and carnelian. And the glow of an emerald circled his throne like a rainbow.

REVELATION 4:2-3

THE SCENE PORTRAYED in this Scripture takes place in the present Heaven. Some argue that the New Earth shouldn't be called Heaven. But Heaven, by definition, is God's special dwelling place. And in Revelation 21:3, we're told that God's home will be "among his people" on the New Earth. Heaven is where God's throne is, and "the throne of God and of the Lamb will be there" (Revelation 22:3). With God's presence and throne both on the New Earth, it will be the Heaven on Earth we have always dreamed of!

RESURRECTED PEOPLE
LIVING ON A RESURRECTED EARTH

I saw a new heaven and a new earth. . . .
And I saw the holy city, the new Jerusalem, coming down from
God out of heaven like a bride beautifully dressed for her husband.

REVELATION 21:1-2

GOD DIDN'T MAKE A MISTAKE when He formed the first human being from the dust of the earth. And He wasn't speaking metaphorically when He said He wanted humanity to live on Earth and rule it: "God blessed them and said, 'Be fruitful and multiply. Fill the earth and govern it. Reign over the fish in the sea, the birds in the sky, and all the animals that scurry along the ground'" (Genesis 1:28). God has not abandoned His original design and plan. One day, He will restore what was corrupted by sin and bring the present Heaven down to the New Earth. That's where He invites each of us to come and live with Him forever!

The angel also showed me the river of the water of life,

sparkling like crystal, and coming from the throne of God

and of the Lamb and flowing down the middle of the city's street.

On each side of the river was the tree of life, which bears fruit twelve times a year,

once each month; and its leaves are for the healing of the nations.

REVELATION 22:1-2, GNT

HUMANKIND WAS EVICTED from Eden, but Eden was not destroyed. The same tree of life that existed in Eden exists now in the present Heaven: "To everyone who is victorious I will give fruit from the tree of life in the paradise of God" (Revelation 2:7). We're also told in Revelation that the heart of Eden, the tree of life, will be located in the New Jerusalem that is brought down to the New Earth. Because the tree will grow on both banks of a great river, it will either have massive roots that span its breadth or become a forest of life. And since we know the tree that distinguished Eden will be there, why not Eden itself? The original Eden may even be a great park at the center of the New Jerusalem! Perhaps we'll go there and hear Adam and Eve tell their stories.

-8-

THE NEW JERUSALEM—
A RESERVOIR OF WEALTH AND TREASURE

The foundations of the city walls were decorated with…jasper…
sapphire…agate…emerald…onyx…ruby…chrysolite…
beryl…topaz…turquoise…jacinth…amethyst.
The twelve gates were twelve pearls, each gate made of a single pearl.
the great street of the city was of gold, as pure as transparent glass.

REVELATION 21:19-21, NIV

THE NEW JERUSALEM will be the largest city ever, containing extrava-
gant beauty and natural wonders—a vast Eden, integrated with the best of
human culture, under the reign of Christ. Its precious stones and gold repre-
sent incredible wealth, showing the exorbitant riches of God's splendor and
majesty. More wealth than has been accumulated in all history will be spread
freely across this immense city. As we explore the New Earth's capital city, we'll
worship God with awe and wonder!

- 9 -

ETERNAL FREEDOM FROM SORROW

With eager hope, the creation looks forward to the day when
it will join God's children in glorious freedom from death and decay.
For we know that all creation has been groaning as in
the pains of childbirth right up to the present time.

ROMANS 8:20-22

DON'T YOU LONG for the coming redemption? Look at the faces of the people around you; listen to the cries of animals, to the roar of the ocean, to the wind in the trees. Do you sense an intense longing for something better—for the world to be made right at last? Note that in the Scripture above, Paul doesn't use analogies of death and destruction, but of childbirth: What was brought down by the Fall will be restored and uplifted to its original condition. Things will no longer get worse, but only better. The best of bodies, minds, culture, and nature awaits us in the coming world.

LASTING REST AFTER OUR PRESENT HARDSHIPS

I heard a voice from Heaven, saying, "Write this!
From henceforth happy are the dead who die in the Lord!"
"Happy indeed," says the Spirit, "for they rest from
their labours and their deeds go with them!"

REVELATION 14:13, *PHILLIPS*

FTER GOD CREATED THE WORLD, He rested on the seventh day (Genesis 2:2). For Adam and Eve, Eden was a picture of rest—offering not only sleep and leisure, but also meaningful and enjoyable work, abundant food, natural beauty, and unhindered friendship with God and each other. Yet even with Eden's perfection, one day was still set aside for special rest. God prescribed it for Adam and Eve before they sinned, and He prescribed it for the entire sin-tainted human race who followed. On the New Earth, work will be refreshing, yet regular times of renewal will continue to be built into our lives. Wouldn't it be wise to practice the art of worshipful rest now?

-11-

The doors were locked; but suddenly, as before, Jesus was standing among them. "Peace be with you," he said. Then he said to Thomas, "Put your finger here, and look at my hands. Put your hand into the wound in my side. Don't be faithless any longer. Believe!"

JOHN 20:26-27

SOME SUPPOSE THAT IN HEAVEN we'll forget that we were once desperate sinners. But if that were the case, how could we appreciate the depth and meaning of Christ's sacrificial death? No, we'll never forget that our sins nailed Jesus to the cross, since Christ's resurrected body still has nail-scarred hands and feet. Even though God will wipe away the tears and sorrow attached to this present life, He will not erase from our minds Christ's redemptive work for us. Heaven's happiness will be enhanced by our memories and our informed appreciation of God's glorious grace, for which we will continually give Him thanks.

12

There is joy in the presence of God's angels when even one sinner repents.

LUKE 15:10

WHEN SOMEONE ON EARTH becomes a believer in Christ, joy erupts in Heaven, where God's saints are living right now among angels. God, His angels, and His redeemed children all rejoice together. Many assume that people in Heaven must not be aware of anything that is happening on Earth; otherwise, they couldn't be happy. But they're not frail beings whose joy can be preserved only if they are shielded from what's really going on in the universe. If they rejoice over people on Earth who put their faith in Jesus, they must be aware, to some extent, of what's happening here, as Revelation 6:9-10 shows. Happiness in Heaven isn't based on ignorance, but on perspective. God's happiness is the prevailing mood of Heaven, and nothing witnessed on Earth can derail it.

-13-

SEEKING HEAVEN AND GETTING EARTH THROWN IN

*They were looking for a better place, a heavenly homeland. That is why God
is not ashamed to be called their God, for he has prepared a city for them.*

HEBREWS 11:16

*Set your sights on the realities of heaven,
where Christ sits in the place of honor at God's right hand.
Think about the things of heaven, not the things of earth.*

COLOSSIANS 3:1-2

WE'RE COMMANDED to set our hearts on Heaven. To long for Christ is to long for Heaven, for that's where we'll live with Him. Yet we're unaccustomed to heavenly thinking since our minds are occupied with earthly matters. So we must work at it. Just as a shepherd looks for his lost sheep (Matthew 18:12) and a merchant searches for fine pearls (Matthew 13:45), our pursuit of God's Kingdom should be diligent, active, and single-minded. If you're going to spend the next lifetime on the New Earth, why not spend this lifetime with that in mind? As you eagerly anticipate and prepare for your eternal life, your experience on this present Earth will be enriched.

14

Your gates will always stand open, they will never be shut, day or night,
so that people may bring you the wealth of the nations—
their kings led in triumphal procession. . . .
I will make you the everlasting pride and the joy of all generations.

ISAIAH 60:11, 15, NIV

ON THE NEW EARTH, the nations and kings will bring their greatest treasures into a renewed and glorious Jerusalem. Those from "every nation and tribe and people and language" (Revelation 7:9) will participate. When they bring their treasures into this magnificent city, it will usher in a time of unprecedented rejoicing for all God's people. Most of us are unaccustomed to thinking of nations, rulers, civilizations, and cultures as aspects of Heaven, but Isaiah 60 is one of many passages demonstrating that the New Earth will in fact be *earthly*.

- 15 -

*He took me in the Spirit to a great, high mountain, and he showed
me the holy city, Jerusalem, descending out of heaven from God.
It shone with the glory of God and sparkled like a precious
stone—like jasper as clear as crystal.*

REVELATION 21:10-11

WE CAN LEARN A LOT about people by walking through their houses. In the redeemed creation, the whole universe will be God's house—and the New Jerusalem will be His living room. Heaven's capital will be filled with natural wonders, magnificent architecture, and thriving culture—but it will have no crime, pollution, sirens, traffic fatalities, garbage, or homelessness. Imagine enjoying this beautiful city without pickpockets, porn shops, drugs, or prostitution. The Artist's fingerprints will be seen everywhere: The priceless stones will speak of His beauty and grandeur, the open gates of His accessibility and hospitality, and the shining light of His majestic holiness. God will delight in sharing with us the glories of His—and our—capital city of the new creation!

EARTH'S PRESENT BEAUTY: JUST A HINT OF WHAT'S TO COME

(The seraphim) were calling out to each other,
"Holy, holy, holy is the LORD of Heaven's Armies!
The whole earth is filled with his glory!"

ISAIAH 6:3

BECAUSE EARTH WAS DAMAGED BY SIN, we have never known a world without corruption, suffering, and death. Yet we yearn for such a life and such a world. When we see a roaring waterfall, beautiful flowers, a wild animal in its native habitat, or the joy in the eyes of our pets when they see us, we sense that this world is—or at least *was meant to be*—our home. If we want to know what the ultimate Heaven and our eternal home will be like, *the best place to start is by looking around us.* The present Earth is as much a valid reference point for envisioning the New Earth as our present bodies are for envisioning our new bodies.

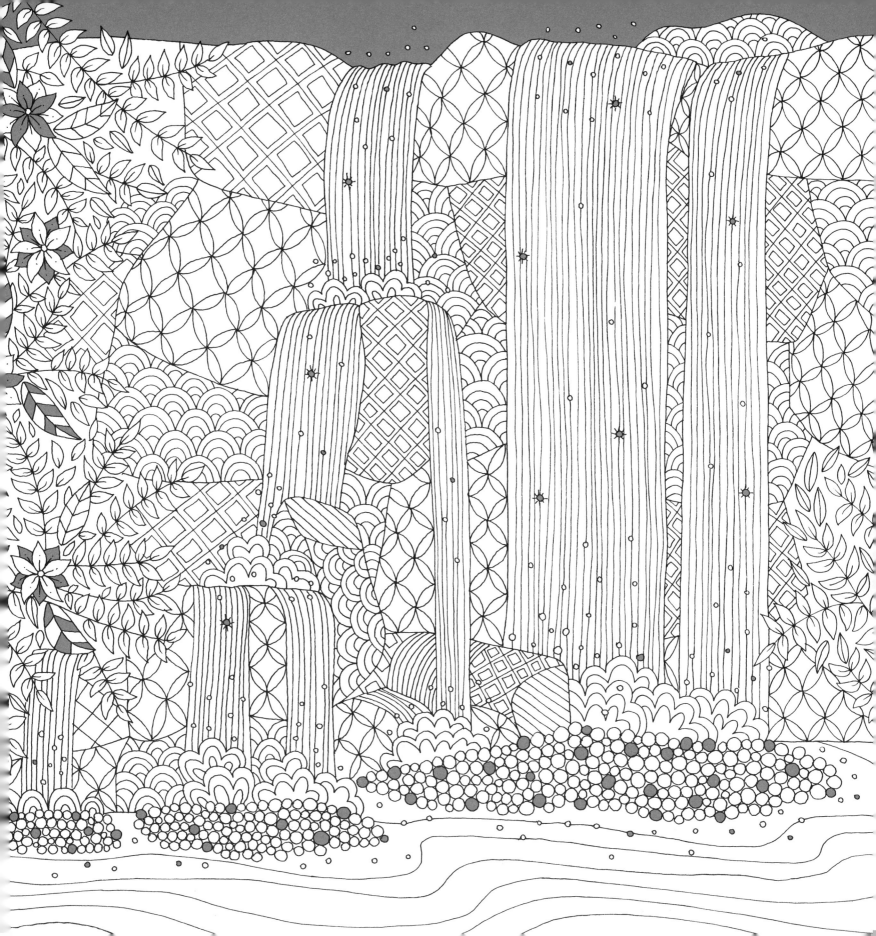

-17-

SEE THE SEA IN A WHOLE NEW WAY

The wealth on the seas will be brought to you,
to you the riches of the nations will come.

ISAIAH 60:5, NIV

As SOMEONE WHO LOVES TO SNORKEL and marvel at multicolored fish, great sea turtles, dolphins, seals, rays, and eels, I sympathize with people's resistance to the words "no longer any sea" in Revelation 21:1 (NIV). Many Bible scholars, Charles Spurgeon among them, believe this actually means an end to all the shipwrecks, drownings, flooding, poisoned salt water, and death associated with the oceans under the Curse. Certainly this passage doesn't say there won't be large bodies of water. Revelation tells us a great river will flow through the New Jerusalem (22:1-2). Flowing rivers go somewhere, so we might expect that the New Earth could have, if not oceans exactly as we now know them, vast sea-like lakes brimming with life. Since the psalmist celebrates "the fish in the sea, and everything that swims the ocean currents" (Psalm 8:7-9), I believe that on the New Earth we'll swim, dive, and play with God's creatures of the deep!

WEATHER ON THE NEW EARTH? WHY NOT!

I will bless my people and their homes around my holy hill.
And in the proper season I will send the showers they need. There will be
showers of blessing. The orchards and fields of my people will yield bumper crops.

EZEKIEL 34:26-27

SOME PEOPLE HAVE NEVER THOUGHT about weather in the afterlife, often because they don't believe that after death they'll live in a physical place again. Or if they think of the New Earth at all, they don't think of it as a real Earth. They assume there will be no sunshine or weather patterns because of Scriptures like Revelation 21:23: "The city has no need of sun or moon, for the glory of God illuminates the city." Yet in this passage, the emphasis isn't on the elimination of sun and moon, but on their being overshadowed by the greater light of God. Are rain and snow bad? No! "The rain and snow . . . cause the grain to grow, producing seed for the farmer and bread for the hungry" (Isaiah 55:10). Will rain turn to snow in higher elevations on the New Earth? Sure—who can say it won't? If there's snow, will people throw snowballs and ski? Of course. I love winter's blankets of snow. Fall's crisp air and brilliant colors. Spring's fresh, erupting beauty. Summer's mellow warmth. Will there be seasons on the New Earth? I can't think of a single reason why not!

AT LAST, WE'LL HAVE TIME FOR EVERYTHING

Let us be glad and rejoice, and let us give honor to him. For the time has come for the wedding feast of the Lamb, and his bride has prepared herself.

REVELATION 19:7

THE PHRASE "TIME SHALL BE NO MORE" is found in an old hymn. Despite its use in a few older Bible translations, it doesn't reflect the meaning of Revelation 10:6, which speaks of no more delay in the fulfillment of God's eternal plan. There actually *is* time in the present Heaven (Revelation 8:1), and there will be time on the New Earth—Revelation 22:2 says that the tree of life will produce a fresh crop of fruit each month. People imagine time is an enemy because the clock seems to move slowly when we're having a root canal and quickly when we're doing what we love. But time isn't the problem—the Curse is. Once the Curse has ended, as God promises it will (Revelation 22:3), time will never work against us. On the New Earth, time will always bring us gain, not loss—and we won't run out of it. It will extend happiness, not suffering. It will draw us closer not to death but to God, who is Life. The passing of time will bring new adventures that need not end. When we see God face-to-face, time will pass, but we'll be lost in Him. We'll delight in time because it's part of what God calls "very good."

The time has come for the wedding feast of the Lamb, and his bride has prepared herself.

REVELATION 19:7

SPEND ETERNITY EXPLORING CREATION WITH JESUS

Father, I want those you have given me to be with me
where I am, and to see my glory, the glory you have given me
because you loved me before the creation of the world.

JOHN 17:24, NIV

HAVE YOU EVER IMAGINED what it would be like to walk the earth with Jesus, just as the disciples did? If you know Christ, you will have that opportunity—on the New Earth. The infinitely fascinating God of the universe is by far the most important and most interesting person we'll ever meet. Jesus is God, so whatever we do with Jesus, we'll be doing with God! What will it be like to run beside Jesus as together you explore the renewed creation? Can you picture yourself laughing, singing, swimming, and playing catch with the God-man? Jesus even promised we will eat and drink with Him in His Kingdom (Luke 22:30)!

GET READY TO JOIN THE FEAST

In Jerusalem, the LORD of Heaven's Armies will spread a wonderful

feast for all the people of the world. It will be a delicious banquet with clear,

well-aged wine and choice meat. There he will remove the cloud of gloom,

the shadow of death that hangs over the earth. He will swallow up death forever!

The Sovereign LORD will wipe away all tears. . . . In that day

the people will proclaim, "This is our God! We trusted in him, and he saved us!

This is the LORD, in whom we trusted. Let us rejoice in the salvation he brings!"

ISAIAH 25:6-9

WHAT DO PEOPLE DO AT ANY FEAST? They talk, tell stories, celebrate, laugh, and enjoy amazing food and desserts. How much more so at Christ's wedding feast! Imagine sitting down to eat and raising glasses to toast the King. On the New Earth, will we always be on our faces at Christ's feet, worshiping Him? No, because Scripture says we'll be doing many other things—living in dwelling places, sharing meals together, reigning with Christ, and working for Him. Though we won't always kneel, *all that we do will be an act of worship*; we will eat and drink and do everything to His glory (1 Corinthians 10:31). We'll enjoy full and unbroken fellowship with Christ!

DELIGHTING IN REDEEMED CULTURE

The nations will walk by (the New Jerusalem's) light,

and the kings of the earth will bring their glory into it. The city's gates shall stand open

day after day.... Into the city they will bring the splendours and honours of the nations.

But nothing unclean, no one who deals in filthiness and lies, shall ever at any

time enter it—only those whose names are written in the Lamb's book of life.

REVELATION 21:24-27, *PHILLIPS*

GOD CREATED US AS HIS IMAGE-BEARERS to glorify Him in innovative accomplishments. Even after the Fall, Scripture describes developments in ranching, the playing of musical instruments, and metallurgy (Genesis 4:20-22). None of the negative, sin-tainted by-products of civilization, like pollution, materialism, and pornography, are intrinsic to human culture. That's because culture is the natural, God-intended product of His gifting, equipping, and calling for humankind to rule over creation. On the New Earth, the nations will bring their splendors— likely handcrafted—and present them to the King. Jesus is pro-culture: He's the creative Artist behind and over it, and He will forever redeem it.

Into the city they will bring the splendours and honours of the nations.

REVELATION 21:26

23

Many will come from the east and the west, and will take their places at the feast with Abraham, Isaac and Jacob in the kingdom of heaven.

MATTHEW 8:11, NIV

ALONG WITH GREAT FOOD like breads, nuts, fruits and vegetables, fruit juice from the tree of life, water, and wine, is there any reason to suppose we won't drink coffee or tea on the New Earth? If coffee beans and tea leaves were some of God's good ideas for the old Earth, why not the new one? Can you imagine enjoying a cup of coffee with Jesus? If you can't, why not? Those who suffer from food allergies, weight problems, or addictions can look forward to enjoying every good thing to eat and drink on the New Earth. To be liberated from sin, death, and bondage on the New Earth won't mean enjoying *fewer* pleasures, but *more*. We may not yet have tasted our favorite food or drink—and if we have, it will taste even better in God's everlasting Kingdom!

LIONS AND LAMBS WILL BE OUR GENTLE COMPANIONS

Look! I am creating new heavens and a new earth....
Be glad; rejoice forever in my creation! And look!
I will create Jerusalem as a place of happiness.
Her people will be a source of joy.... The wolf and the lamb will feed together.
The lion will eat hay like a cow.

ISAIAH 65:17-18, 25

WE KNOW THAT GOD WILL FASHION the New Earth with fruit, trees, and renewed bodies of water for His children to enjoy. So why wouldn't we expect Him to include renewed animals? Lions, wolves, and lambs will live there, as well as leopards, goats, and calves (Isaiah 11:6). It appears God won't withhold what He gave Adam and Eve in Eden for delight and companionship. Rather than revoking His decision to put animals and people together, God will fulfill His original design on the New Earth, where fear and suffering will no longer exist. All living beings will together enjoy our Creator and Redeemer and His fantastic new universe!

-25-

WILL WE REUNITE WITH OUR BELOVED PETS?

What we suffer now is nothing compared to the glory he will reveal to us later.
For all creation is waiting eagerly for that future day when God will reveal who his
children really are. Against its will, all creation was subjected to God's curse.
But with eager hope, the creation looks forward to the day when it will
join God's children in glorious freedom from death and decay.

ROMANS 8:18-21

GOD LOVES TO GIVE GOOD GIFTS to His children (Matthew 7:9-11). So if it would make you happy to have one or more of your pets with you on the New Earth, that may be a good enough reason for God to make it happen. He could (1) create entirely new animals; (2) bring animals back to life, giving them new bodies that will last forever; or (3) create brand-new animals *and* bring some old ones back to life. Romans 8:21 says that even nonhuman creation looks forward to being raised with God's children—what could that be if not animals? Only God knows for sure what He plans to do. But wouldn't it be just like Him to recreate the same pets He entrusted to us in this life? What a delightful reunion that would be! As the animal kingdom fell on the coattails of humanity, so it will rise with our redemption on a resurrected Earth.

MAYBE WE'LL SEE EXTINCT ANIMALS COME TO LIFE

Take a look at Behemoth, which I made, just as I made you.

It eats grass like an ox. See its powerful loins and the muscles of its belly.

Its tail is as strong as a cedar. The sinews of its thighs are knit tightly together.

Its bones are tubes of bronze. Its limbs are bars of iron.

It is a prime example of God's handiwork.

JOB 40:15-19

SCRIPTURE SPEAKS of "the time for the final restoration of all things" (Acts 3:21). Will "all things" include extinct animals? Why not? Animals are created for God's glory. God Himself points out to Job how His greatness is revealed in the awesome Behemoth, which many believe is actually a brontosaurus. Picture *Jurassic Park* with all of the awesome majesty of those huge creatures but none of their violence and hostility. Envision riding a triceratops—or flying on the back of a pterodactyl! By resurrecting the long-deceased inhabitants of His original creation, God may show the totality of His victory over sin and death.

NO BOREDOM IN HEAVEN

"Well done!" the king exclaimed.
"You are a good servant. You have been faithful with the little
I entrusted to you, so you will be governor of ten cities as your reward."

LUKE 19:17

*I*F YOU THINK THAT LIFE in God's new universe will be boring, *you're just not getting it!* Consider the flowers that botanists will study (and enjoy), the animals that zoologists will research (and romp with). Gifted astronomers may travel from star system to star system and galaxy to galaxy studying the wonders of God's creation. A disembodied existence would be boring, but our resurrection to bodily life on the New Earth will forever put boredom to death. *Lord, forgive us for embracing one of Satan's favorite heresies—that Heaven will be boring!* No, just the opposite: It will be captivating and exciting. Let's share this with everyone, embracing the fact that both Jesus *and the place He's preparing for us* are Good News!

"You are a GOOD SERVANT. You have been faithful WITH THE LITTLE I entrusted to you, SO YOU WILL BE GOVERNOR of TEN CITIES as your reward."

LUKE 19:17

-28-

All athletes are disciplined in their training.
They do it to win a prize that will fade away, but we do it for an eternal prize.

1 CORINTHIANS 9:25

Whether you eat or drink, or whatever you do, do it all for the glory of God.

1 CORINTHIANS 10:31

WHAT KINDS OF NEW SPORTS might we engage in on the New Earth? The possibilities are limitless. If you've always wished you could hit a home run or kick a football between goalposts, perhaps you'll get to do that. Sports bring out the best in some and the worst in others now, but in the new creation there will be no worst to bring out! I can't think of a single good reason to believe sports won't be part of our resurrected lives. We can expect to see most of the sports we enjoy now, with everyone healthy enough to participate. Perhaps we'll enjoy activities that were once too risky. Imagine snowboarding down the slopes of the New Mount Everest or the New Alps! Maybe you'll play games with your favorite Christian athlete. Your preferred sport in Heaven may be one that you've never played in this life—or that hasn't even been invented yet!

ALL ATHLETES ARE *disciplined* IN THEIR *training*. THEY DO IT TO WIN A *prize* THAT WILL *fade away*, BUT *we do it* FOR AN ETERNAL PRIZE.

I CORINTHIANS 9:25

-29-

WILL WE TRAVEL TO GALAXIES FAR, FAR AWAY?

We are looking forward to the new heavens and new earth
he has promised, a world filled with God's righteousness.

2 PETER 3:13

MANY OF US HAVE ENJOYED the pleasures of traveling this planet. People journey across oceans and to outer space because God made us with the desire to explore and the creativity to make that desire a reality. What will it be like to travel in God's new universe, when we are all the more creative, without the curse of death to hold us back? Ever since I was a child and first glimpsed the Andromeda Galaxy through my telescope, I've wanted to go there. The Bible's promise of new heavens suggests there will be a New Andromeda Galaxy, so I think it's likely that one day I will visit it—to the praise and glory of King Jesus!

66

30

This is the way to have eternal life—to know you,
the only true God, and Jesus Christ, the one you sent to earth.

JOHN 17:3

Since everything God created is good,
we should not reject any of it but receive it with thanks.
For we know it is made acceptable by the word of God and prayer.

1 TIMOTHY 4:4-5

OUR PRIMARY HAPPINESS in Heaven will be knowing and seeing God. Every other joy will be derivative, flowing from the fountain of our relationship with Him. God "richly gives us all we need for our enjoyment" (1 Timothy 6:17), so we should never classify our secondary joys as separate from Him. Flowers are beautiful because God is beautiful. Rainbows are stunning because God is stunning. Puppies are delightful because God is delightful. Sports and amusement parks are fun because God is fun. Though preoccupation with God-given gifts can turn into idolatry, enjoying those same gifts with grateful hearts draws us closer to Him. In Heaven, we'll have no capacity for idolatry. Whenever we find joy in God's gifts, we'll always find joy in Him.

31

GOD TAKES PLEASURE IN GIVING US HIS GIFTS

*Do not be afraid, little flock, for your Father has
been pleased to give you the kingdom.*

LUKE 12:32, NIV

IN HEAVEN, we'll bask in God's constant presence. Freed from sin, we'll never have to worry about putting people or things above God. Sometimes we wrongly conclude that pleasures are bad for us, forgetting that it was God Himself who made them. God is not up in Heaven frowning at us and saying, "Stop it—you should find joy only in Me." This would be as foreign to our heavenly Father's nature as it would be to mine as an earthly father if I gave my daughters Christmas gifts and then pouted because they enjoyed them too much. No, I am *delighted* when my children and grandchildren enjoy the presents I've given them! Their pleasure in my gifts draws us closer together.

32

SERVICE AND WORK AS THEY WERE MEANT TO BE

*No longer will there be any curse. The throne of God
and of the Lamb will be in the city, and his servants will serve him.*

REVELATION 22:3, NIV

*S*ERVE IS A VERB, and servants are people who are active and occupied—with things to do, places to go, and people to see. God Himself is a worker. He didn't create the world and then retire. Consider Christ's activities as a carpenter and later as an itinerant preacher: fishing, sailing, meeting people, talking, teaching, eating—connecting with His disciples and doing His life's work. The idea of working in Heaven is foreign to many; but God gave work to Adam and Eve as a gift—it wasn't part of the Curse. Rather, the Curse made work menial, tedious, and frustrating. On the New Earth, work will be redeemed and transformed into what God intended!

WORK

CARE

GLORY TO GOD

SATISFACTION

CHARACTER FAITHFULNESS FULFILLMENT

UNIVERSAL PEACE AND UNITY

Glory to God in highest heaven,
and peace on earth to those with whom God is pleased.

LUKE 2:14

WE SHOULDN'T WAIT UNTIL HEAVEN to seek reconciliation with those of different ethnicities or backgrounds and estranged friends, family, or church members. Scripture commands us to "work at living in peace with everyone" (Hebrews 12:14). As Christ-followers, through our mutual loyalty to our common King—a loyalty that transcends our differences and is enriched by them—we can gain a foretaste of the perfect unity we'll experience in Heaven. Christ's work on the cross put racism to death: "He himself is our peace, who has made the two groups one and has destroyed the barrier, the dividing wall of hostility" (Ephesians 2:14, NIV). On the New Earth, the work of reconciliation will be complete, and we'll celebrate our unified diversity by singing praise to Jesus that His blood "has ransomed people for God from every tribe and language and people and nation" (Revelation 5:9).

-34-

HOSPITALITY AS WE'VE NEVER KNOWN IT BEFORE

Use worldly wealth to gain friends for yourselves,
so that when it is gone, you will be welcomed into eternal dwellings.

LUKE 16:9, NIV

JESUS SPOKE OF "ETERNAL DWELLINGS"—places where we'll stay and enjoy fellowship with friends, perhaps as we move about the heavenly Kingdom. These "friends" are likely those whose lives we've touched on Earth through our giving of money and time. Some friends will be new ones—those who benefited at a distance from our prayers and generosity. But surely many will be people we already know, people whose lives we've invested in. Do I believe Jesus is suggesting we'll actually share lodging, meals, and fellowship with friends in God's Kingdom? Yes. Sound far-fetched? Some mistakenly believe that Heaven won't be earthlike, but Scripture is clear: Resurrected people will inhabit a resurrected Earth, live in dwelling places, and share rich hospitality.

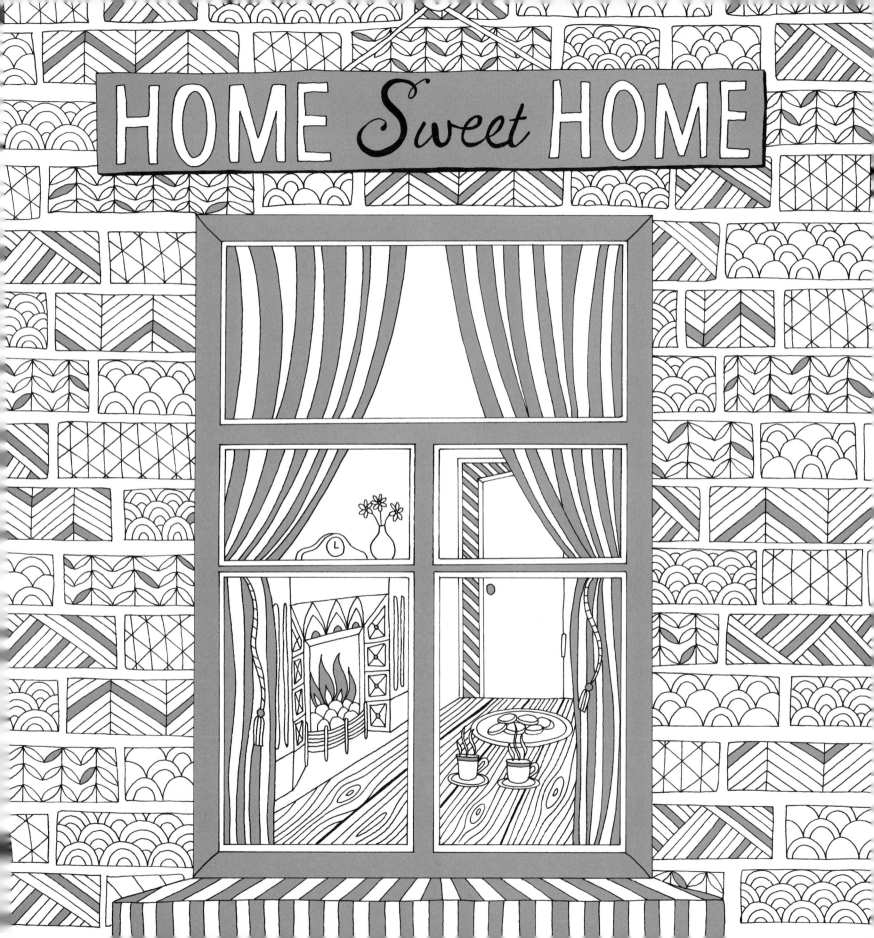

DANCE AND SING LIKE NOBODY'S WATCHING

*The voice I heard was like the sound of harpists playing
on their harps, and they were singing a new song before the throne.*

REVELATION 14:2-3, ESV

*Then young women of Israel will be happy and dance,
the young men and old men also. I will change their sadness into happiness;
I will give them comfort and joy instead of sadness.*

JEREMIAH 31:13, NCV

SCRIPTURE INFORMS US that music is a part of life in the present Heaven, and we should certainly expect to find plenty of it on the New Earth as well. As a musical novice, I might eventually compose something worthy of Bach. And what kind of music do you suppose Bach will compose? There will also be dancing! Throughout the ages, God's people—including Miriam and King David—have celebrated and worshiped with dancing. God created us with the ability to dance and make music. Even those of us who are presently tone-deaf or have "two left feet" can still honor God with our worship, all while looking forward to new singing, dancing, or instrumental skills that will last forever. "Praise the LORD, for the LORD is good; celebrate his lovely name with music" (Psalm 135:3).

LAUGH

-36-

Happy are you who hunger now, because you will be satisfied.
Happy are you who weep now, because you will laugh.

LUKE 6:21, CEB

GOD CREATED ALL GOOD THINGS, including humor. If God didn't have a sense of humor, we wouldn't either, since He designed us in His likeness. You don't think human beings invented play and happiness, do you? In Heaven, I think Jesus will laugh with us, maybe loudest of all. His fun-loving nature may be our greatest source of laughter. In the midst of this life's trials and difficulties, Jesus says we should "leap for joy" as we anticipate the heavenly rewards to come (Luke 6:23). Can you imagine someone leaping for joy in silence? Listen to any group of people who are celebrating together, and what do you hear? Laughter! Let's front-load eternity's heartfelt laughter into our lives today.

·37·

HUMBLE WORKERS WILL GAIN RICH REWARDS

Happy are those who know they are spiritually poor;
the Kingdom of heaven belongs to them!

MATTHEW 5:3, GNT

LOOK AROUND YOU TO SEE the meek and humble. They may include custodians, locksmiths' assistants, bus drivers, and moms who spend their days at home changing diapers, doing laundry, packing lunches, drying tears, and driving in car pools. I once gave one of my books to a delightful hotel bellman who prayed for the Christian conference I was speaking at and went out of his way to help us. He seemed stunned, overwhelmed. With tears he said, "You didn't need to do that. I'm only a bellman." This brother had spent his life serving other people. There was no "only" about him. It might very well be someone like him that I'll have the privilege of serving under in God's Kingdom. Who will be the kings of the New Earth? I think that bellman will be one of them. And I'll be honored to carry his bags.

-38-

OUR BEST EFFORTS MAY FIND A PLACE IN THE NEW CREATION

(Jesus) must remain in heaven until the time for the final restoration
of all things, as God promised long ago through his holy prophets.

ACTS 3:21

SINCE JESUS WILL RESURRECT His people and the natural world, might He also, in "the final restoration of all things" resurrect a song or book written to His glory? A letter that encouraged a friend or stranger? A quilt stitched for an orphan child or a baseball bat handcrafted as a gift for a grandson's birthday? Restoring such things may seem trivial. But the opposite is true: It emphasizes Christ's power to radically renew the human race—and far more. We know for certain that Heaven makes good deeds permanent in the "scroll of remembrance" (Malachi 3:16) and secures treasures in Heaven sent ahead through giving (Matthew 6:20). Whether or not God chooses to resurrect precious memorabilia from this life, we know for certain that He cherishes the good works He created us to do (Ephesians 2:10).

-39-

NO MORE PAIN, TEARS, OR DEATH

Where, O death, is your victory? Where, O death, is your sting?

1 CORINTHIANS 15:55, NIV

He will wipe every tear from their eyes,
and there will be no more death or sorrow or crying or pain.

REVELATION 21:4

OUR PAIN AND SUFFERING may or may not be relieved in this life, but they will certainly be relieved in the life to come. That is Christ's promise— no more pain or death! He will wipe away all our tears. Jesus took on our sorrows so that one day we would be free from them all. By meditating on Heaven and learning to look forward to living there, we don't eliminate our suffering, but we can at least alleviate some pain and put it in perspective. Suffering and death are temporary. Thanks to Jesus, those who trust Him will inherit eternal life and health!

ANTICIPATING OUR HEAVENLY REWARDS

If anyone gives even a cup of cold water to one of these little ones because he is my disciple, I tell you the truth, he will certainly not lose his reward.

MATTHEW 10:42, NIV

You have caused them to become a Kingdom of priests for our God. And they will reign on the earth.

REVELATION 5:10

ON THE NEW EARTH, we'll forever be with the Person we were made for, in a place made for us. In proportion to their service, some will reign with Christ and be granted leadership over cities (Luke 19:17). God's people will even command angels (1 Corinthians 6:3)! Scripture refers to five different crowns God gives His sons and daughters, each suggesting a leadership position (James 1:12; 1 Corinthians 9:24-25; Philippians 4:1; 1 Peter 5:1-4; and 2 Timothy 4:6-8). Jesus keeps track of even our smallest acts of kindness, including offering a cup of water to a fellow believer. He's eager to reward us for our service. May He say to each one of us, "Well done, good and faithful servant! You have been faithful with a few things; I will put you in charge of many things. Come and share your master's happiness!" (Matthew 25:23, NIV).

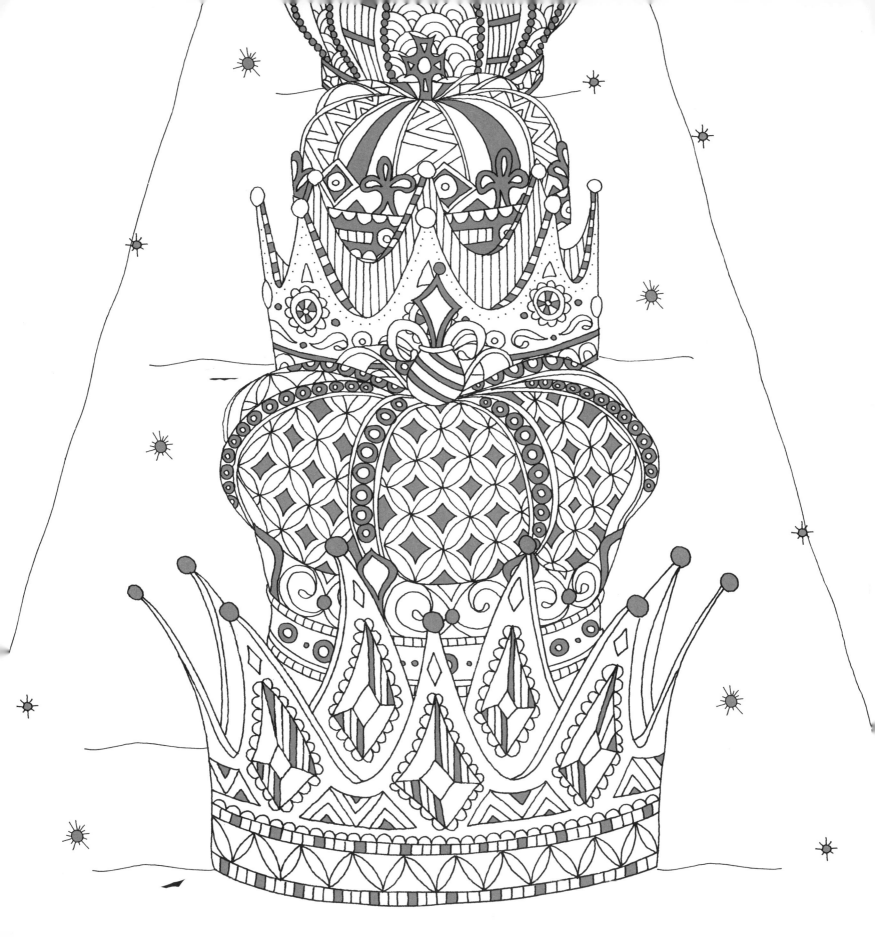

ACKNOWLEDGMENTS

CONSIDERABLE TIME was invested by many to produce this book. After I submitted the idea, Tyndale House's Becky Brandvik spearheaded the project with grace and efficiency. Then I called on Doreen Button, who chose and edited selections from works I've written about Heaven, which I then revised. Doreen also proposed most of the visual concepts. Anisa Baker served as editor at Tyndale House along with Carolyn Ingermanson as copyeditor, and art director Jennifer Ghionzoli worked with artists Lizzie Preston and Jennifer Tucker, who did a wonderful job. Stephanie Anderson, with Eternal Perspective Ministries, also edited. This was a team effort from the beginning. I'm deeply grateful for everyone involved, and I'm especially thankful to the Master Artist, who will redeem what's broken and bring into full flower the new heavens and New Earth we have sought to celebrate.

WE FIX OUR EYES NOT ON WHAT IS SEEN, BUT ON WHAT

IS UNSEEN. FOR WHAT IS SEEN IS TEMPORARY, BUT

what is unseen is Eternal

2 CORINTHIANS 4:18

 epm eternal perspective ministries

with author Randy Alcorn

Eternal Perspective Ministries is a Bible-believing, Christ-centered nonprofit organization founded and directed by Randy Alcorn.

We're dedicated to:

- teaching principles of God's Word, emphasizing an eternal viewpoint;
- assisting the church in ministering to the unreached, unfed, unborn, uneducated, unreconciled, and unsupported people around the world.

Since its inception in 1990, EPM has given over seven million dollars in book royalties to ministries around the world. We love the fact that God uses Randy's books to change people's lives in two ways: through the reading of the words and through the giving away of the royalties.

*Visit **www.epm.org** to learn more about EPM, access free resources, and read Randy's blog; browse books and products at **www.epm.org/books**.*

Follow Randy and EPM

RANDY ALCORN

Contact Us

Online at www.epm.org

503.668.5200 | Toll-free 1.877.376.4567

39085 Pioneer Blvd, Suite 206, Sandy, OR 97055

f facebook.com/
randyalcorn

🐦 twitter.com/
randyalcorn

ETERNAL PERSPECTIVE MINISTRIES

RANDY ALCORN is an author and the founder and director of Eternal Perspective Ministries (EPM), a nonprofit organization dedicated to teaching principles of God's Word and assisting the church in ministering to unreached, unfed, unborn, uneducated, unreconciled, and unsupported people around the world. His ministry focus is communicating the strategic importance of using our earthly time, money, possessions, and opportunities to invest in need-meeting ministries that count for eternity. He accomplishes this by analyzing, teaching, and applying biblical truth.

Before starting EPM in 1990, Randy served as a pastor for fourteen years. He has a bachelor of theology and a master of arts in biblical studies from Multnomah University and an honorary doctorate from Western Seminary in Portland, Oregon, and has taught on the adjunct faculties of both. A *New York Times* bestselling author, Randy has written more than fifty books, including *Heaven*, *The Treasure Principle*, and the award-winning novel *Safely Home*. His books have sold more than ten million copies and have been translated into more than sixty languages.

Randy has written for many magazines, including EPM's *Eternal Perspectives*. He is active on Facebook and Twitter and has been a guest on more than seven hundred radio, television, and online programs.

Randy resides in Gresham, Oregon, with his wife, Nanci. They have two married daughters and are the proud grandparents of five grandsons. Randy enjoys time spent with his family, biking, snorkeling, underwater photography, researching, and reading.

You may contact Eternal Perspective Ministries at www.epm.org or 39085 Pioneer Blvd., Suite 206, Sandy, OR 97055, or 503-668-5200.

FOLLOW RANDY

FACEBOOK www.facebook.com/randyalcorn

TWITTER www.twitter.com/randyalcorn

and on HIS BLOG www.epm.org/blog

NOTES

LIVING
EXPRESSIONS™
COLLECTION

978-1-4964-2179-1

978-1-4964-1579-0

Bring creative journaling and coloring into your personal
time with God. Filled with more than 100 designs to color,
plenty of space for journaling and sketching, and 40
inspiring prayers, these beautiful gift books will engage
your whole heart in expressing devotion to God!